THE PRISONERS

THE PRISONERS

Poems by Ace Boggess

BRICK ROAD
POETRY PRESS

Cover: The Prison Courtyard (1890) by Vincent van Gogh (1853–1890).
Oil on canvas. The State Pushkin Museum of Fine Arts, Moscow, Russia

Library of Congress Control Number: 2013957154
ISBN-13: 978-0-9835304-7-3

Published by Brick Road Poetry Press
P. O. Box 751
Columbus, GA 31902-0751
www.brickroadpoetrypress.com

Brick Road logo by Dwight New

OTHER BOOKS BY THIS AUTHOR:

The Beautiful Girl Whose Wish Was Not Fulfilled

Wild Sweet Notes II: More Great Poetry from West Virginia (editor)

For Murphy,
and for all those I met along the way
on both sides of the cage

ACKNOWLEDGMENTS

The author wishes to thank the following publications in which these poems first appeared, sometimes in older, somewhat different forms:

ABZ: "Cool, Real Cool"

Atlanta Review: "Prison View" and "Can't You Leave a Man a Little Shred of Dignity?"

Blast Furnace: "The Prisoner's Shadow" and "What Will You Do When You Get Out?"

Bloodroot Literary Magazine: "Apology"

Bluestem: "Wake Up"

Caveat Lector: "The Chaplain at Night"

Clare: "Do You Know You're Being Watched?"

Cloudbank: "Expirations"

Cold Mountain Review: "In Back of the Prison Van"

Common Ground Review: "What's the Worst You've Seen?"

Constellations: "Possible Side Effects"

Cutthroat: "Suppose He Wants to Rob—Who Can Prevent Him?"

The Dos Passos Review: "Security Team"

Ellipsis: "Watching the Steelers Win the Super Bowl"

The Evening Street Review: "The Poker Players"

Front Range Review: "Status Report" and "Do You Feel Like We're Out to Get You?"

Haight Ashbury Literary Journal: "How and Why Did He Get Hooked on *Oxycontin*?"

Heavy Feather Review: "Has the Music Faded at All?"

Iodine Poetry Journal: "The Mask" and "40th Birthday"

J Journal: "Drug History," "Before Prison," "The Rule Breakers" and "Jailhouse Lawyer"

The Listening Eye: "They Didn't Tell You, Did They?"

The Main Street Rag: "Doing Time," "Midnights," "Who Has the Courage to Break Out?" and "And Why Did He, Himself, Feel This Guilt Somewhere Deep Inside Him?"

Mudfish: "The Parameters"

Muse & Stone: "The Institutional Magistrate"

The New Mexico Poetry Review: "What Was Your First Day of Incarceration Like?"

Off the Coast: "Freedom"

Oyez Review: "The Prisoner's Gospel"

Permafrost: "The Prison Chefs"

Pinyon: "Who Can Ever Answer for the Morrow?"

Poem: "So We Know Where We Stand, Don't We?" and "Neither Here Nor There"

Poet Lore: "Flight of Fancy"

RATTLE: "Can They Do That?" and "Property"

Rhino: "Yes"

River Styx: "The Performers"

Sandy River Review: "Was It a Sign of Good Character or a Serious Character Flaw?"

Santa Fe Literary Review: "Creative Writing" and "Release"

Sierra Nevada Review: "So What If Blood Was Spilled?"

SLANT: "Shakedown" and "In the Dayroom"

The South Carolina Review: "Tell Me"

Southern California Review: "Letter to the Parole Board"

Trajectory: "Armed Robbery"

Tribeca Poetry Review: "How Are You Feeling Now?"

Tulane Review: "Letter to My Victim" and "Death Notice"

White Pelican Review: "Thursday"

Wisconsin Review: "Who Can Ever Answer for the Morrow?"

Xavier Review: "What Right Have I to Be Happy?"

CONTENTS

I. Crime and Punishment

II. Notes from the Underground

III. The Idiot

I.

Crime and Punishment

Prison View

First moon in five months
full outside my window
at the Martinsburg Correctional Center
where I've just arrived six hours
from my former jail home.
Same spare walls, spiritless meals,
but new clothes & a new view:
a field of short grass, scrub & dirt
like a nature preserve in Kenya,
vast, unreachable sky, few stars &
moon. I cling to that great dot
in these hardest nights of hardest days.
It warms me with love
like a faded, broken Valentine,
swears, *I'll see you again,*
I'll wait for you, I will....

No Monuments

No Civil War general rides
a horse of algae-green
defending the prison yard.
No granite St. Francis
lowers his head like a circus elephant,
no marble Mary cups a hand
of five-card draw before her eyes &
no colorful cherry Christ
dismounts to walk amongst
the condemned masses. The many
do not look up to see
gnarled, snarling gargoyles
keeping angry watch like stone-
faced guards. No monoliths,
megaliths or obelisks rise
to prick the thousand tearless eyes of God.
No Easter Island faces
smile their many mysteries
around the basketball court &
benches. No milestones
mark the distance traveled,
no weeping matron mourns,
no headstones name
the numbers of the lost.

Thursday

Smiley dances in his state-issued boxers, sings Elvis:
not that jailhouse song, the one about mistrust.

There's the smell of a cigarette's gray, illegal beacon &
hooch in the air like boys playing watermelon football.

Brandon's cussing his old lady on the phone.
Big Man's in the stairwell, punching some snitch in the eye.

It's *West Side Story* without the hot Latina:
what's left is a musical with violence & tragedy.

Then the C.O. can't find his ink pen,
so everyone's locked down.

I take all this in, then lie back on my bunk to read a book
about serial killers & the cops who understand them.

The story makes enough sense that I don't wonder
if there's ever a theme to anything.

Security Team

Picture them playing rock'n'roll,
a band: Big K., wide hands
thumping grooves on the bass guitar;
his buddy, wee & wide-eyed with energy,
soloing, fingering a candy-apple Strat
half his size; Cpl. R. out front,
dark hair down around his eyes,
voicing the microphone—songs his own,
or maybe something older, vintage.
The drummer changes nightly, some-
times men with mad rhythm, others slapdash,
lost in the foggy cul-de-sac of inexperience.
They come on strong with heavy beats,
kinetic passion for the show they put on,
often no more than a walk-through,
roughing out the chords &
keys, but when they're ready,
when they click, it's full concert mode,
playing the lowdown shakedown,
jamming, looking for a sound they hear
in their hearts. They tear apart the stage
like four Pete Townsends dressed in blues.
Listen! *Encore*! Here again
they make their manic music
rife with aggression, white noise,
dancing to that jailhouse rock,
born to be wild, kings of the road,
oh yeah, Johnny, you know
you better be good.

The Prisoner's Gospel

Blessed are the broken,
for they carry their justification
with them like a union card.
Blessed are the first offenders,
for theirs is the kingdom of second chances.
Blessed are the unloved,
for they shall suffer
only for themselves.
Blessed are the flight risks,
for they still have places to go.
Rejoice in influenza, medicated,
sleeping away the days. But
woe unto he who has learned to hope,
for his eyes are stained-glass windows
in a crypt &
woe unto husbands
who see their wives
remembering life without them. Yes &
blessed are the broken &
woe unto the broken &
rejoice in the breaking,
for such men find peace in their pieces,
rebuild themselves: a monument
with scars, a book of the Word
with shattered spine,
duct tape keeping its guts
from the cold stone floor.

Doing Time

Card players throw spades &
curse their misfortunes,
mad coyotes on a moonless night.
Their white tees
reflect fluorescent light,
each a flashbulb firing,
numbers burned across hearts
like five-o'clock shadows.
The Purgatorial pass their time &
time again, less than damned yet
far from the Paradise
of home.

   When I was a boy,
I was innocent once &
bored, afraid, alone.
I circled the world without
leaving the living room: TV-
bound—pizza & sodas
brought to my door like gifts
of misguided magi,
stray lunatics without a god
to praise.

   The phone on the wall
never rings—the sadness
of silence—a false beacon

crashing ships upon invisible
rocks.

        I grew up quiet &
clever, alight with wickedness
that could one day make me
a saint: *Grant me sobriety &*
fidelity, O Lord,
but not today; no,
not until....

        I have watched
the card players finish
their games. I called my wife
between dinner & count,
hearing the safety of her voice,
the hope & promise.
I am a clock that always
points ahead to tomorrow
while my time &
time again pass on
like the fading of hymns
into memory.

Yes

Some days it's difficult to look at the positives.
You wake up with flea bites on your ankle &
by the time sleep comes around again
you've choked down self-pity
at seven times the doctor-recommended dose.
Outside maybe the sun shone at a comfortable setting,
slightly dimmed—just slightly—&
the late-summer wind, warm but subtle,
has carried gifts of stained-glass butterflies
or caramel smells from a nearby traveling carnival.
Perhaps tonight the Perseids will shower you with wishes.
In between you eat well &
sing sweet words to your lover on the phone.
But you're still wearing a blindfold,
smoking a menthol & waiting for the crack
of rifle shot. What do you care if the moon makes a Grail?
For you it's all about the fallings-apart &
centers-not-holding, the woe-is-me,
O Lord, your joyful noise: a great, beaming
Hallelujah of despair.

There Is No End

Unseen, all those stars burn on in the silence of yesterday
& the millions of silences of the millions of yesterdays
it takes to flare & fashion their flush
in the unseen a.m. sky above this prison.

All eyes reach toward tempestuous heavens
only to be reflected by rows of aluminum
that hover like arc lamps over a misty lane.

Night is a time of so much memory
when it should be a time of such forgetting
as to allow a brief repose & freedom.

Though there is stillness, there is still less stillness
than even muffled songs of distant crickets bring.
Oh, to be despised by the universe.... There is no end:
the light resumes before its last flicker fades.

The Prison Chefs

They compile their pizza breads from everything,
composing chromatic symphonies, chaos:

string cheese over garlic loaf, carved sticks of beef &
stir fry, iron ore from meteorites,

the clipped fingernails of God. Into their soups
go saltines & syrup, corn chips, potatoes &

refried beans—an alphabet stew hardened like words &
wrapped in scrolls of papyrus to be swallowed whole

like a bitter brimstone sermon. Their sandwiches,
Sweet Mercy, empty all the commissary shelves:

spice & sausages, pickles, sardines, peanut butter &
cookie crust, whatever mustard & mayo

won't conceal. They're artists; they are ghouls,
making of Renfield a Wolfgang Puck.

They could cook the delight from a birthday cake,
rob it of richness & fill it with rocks, then devour it

brick by painted brick as if redemption might be lost
with any crumb that tumbles from their plate.

The Parameters

fifteen steps
to cross the cell

from steel wall
to steel wall

ten from cage
to window

enough space
to tango

not enough
to race

five doors
two gates

a hundred fifty
miles home

freedom is luxurious
a haven

heaven
of simplicities

without its own

mathematics

not even
the counting

of hours
or of days

Before Prison

I never heard of the potato gun
made with industrial piping &
hairspray to launch its Idaho mortars
past the grassy smell of earth
over moderate mountaintops &
into green fields of someone else's poetry.
I never imagined the cruelty
of seagull genocide achieved by
tossing them fizzy antacid tablets
to burst their guts like the hearts
of so many teenage lovers.
To spark a flame from radio batteries &
razor blades, though sound in science,
hadn't crossed my mind.
Still, I could've done without
seeing what damage boiling water &
hair grease inflict on a face: skin raw &
red as the moon entering its eclipse,
one eye opaque as warm milk
stolen from a baby's bottle. Yes,
men are inventive but, at times,
brutal, ugly beasts: *that* I knew already,
proved with scars on my fingertips,
white lines & darkened blurs: blood
stains the memory of my hands.

The Mask

the ski mask presents a new face
another skull amidst night's glittering catacombs

you wanted to wear the monk's sober hood
but your prayers sound so like curses

menacing mischievous mournful
you carry a sharpened key to the box of blood

scoundrel is a word too good for you
you who'd poison the roots of trees

to bring the honeyed hive into your hands
not just a thief

you have stolen sunlight from the afternoon
pressed your knife's blade to the veins of a cloud

demanding it release
the diamonds from its purse

you're the kind of man the neighbors hardly knew &
yet they knew enough to avoid you

this is what they say of you: a romantic

sensitive & sweet

how in the name of God
could a man hide so much treason with a smile?

Freedom

The color of midnight:
clear & quiescent, scented

with riverbanks, seedheads,
tall grass, life.

Its touch is a woman's,
impassioned & safe

as the sulfur skull
of a foot-long match,

yet sometimes chilly as a lake wind &
covering everything like dust.

It tastes, too,
like charred bacon,

cherries & molasses: a man
would certainly swallow it whole

if he knew its bottle
had a bottom after all.

The Poker Players

On TV, breasty bar girls bring the booze
(smell their vanilla & lavender, their *Passion*,
smell the bourbon straight, Scotch on the rocks).

Familiar faces smile beneath gray Stetsons
or ball caps with logos from *Full Tilt-* &
Absolute Poker- dot com. Cards fly &

chips splash the pot. The prison home edition
has disappeared into a packed casino showroom,
a feeding frenzy of inmates watching

The World Series of Poker on *ESPN*.
The mesmerized cons study the game:
great hands & terrible calls, joy & bluster.

Out of all those famous faces, who will first
misplay a perfect pair of pocket aces?
Can Men Nguyen win? Or, will Scotty Nguyen

bow out saying, "It's all right, baby," while
Daniel Negraneau offers side wagers
on the final rank of Doyle Brunson's kids?

Is there a poker gene? The hereditary gambler?
Everyone watches. Everyone prepares
to test new ploys pitching contraband chips

cut from old decks of cards. They can't all be
poker gods like Johnny Chan, but they can be

lucky for a day, at least—luckier than

others here without a warming flush or
a full house waiting, their existence already
an all-in bet on a locked-in losing hand.

Shakedown

Sometimes dogs marshal the field,
lead wave stalking, hungry as junkies.
Sometimes a force from all directions,

sometimes a team of elites
comes on strong like a barroom
Casanova. Gloved hands roughly

scatter clothes, bed covers, love letters, books &
food. Sometimes a lone scout, probing,
sniffs the air for smoke:

the long shot, loadstone, lone scope
like a camera's lens. Often: shouts, threats &
the silence of guns—voices weightier with menace,

rubber bullets, promises of pain & again
the dogs stinking like wet sand, German shepherds
expressionless as guilty men.

Their throaty tenors never sing,
hearts aflutter for drugs noses crave &,
when they sit, their mute soliloquy

is louder than a squad of Dobermans'
guarded growls or a coyote's
curses for the moon.

Letter to My Victim

Forgive me
for lines opaque
as an egg's
outer innards,
what's called "the white"
but isn't, lines
crooked as a black snake's
broken body on the Interstate;
for promises made
usurping the sovereign
voice of Death;
for wanting more
than a man could possess
without sacrifice &
hard work,
even then.

I'm deeply sorry
in you I saw nothing
human, just a door
through which
hell is exited,
the false paradise
regained. If I could,

I'd take back the knife,
return the blood &
fix your wounds
as though spraying silicon
on a cracked pipe

so we might leave conflicts
for other men

who walk away smiling,
who wash their hands,
who've never looked up
the *Webster's* definition
of regret.

Jailhouse Lawyer

So far none of my clients have been cast
like sacks of mulch into the oubliette;

none drawn, quartered or disemboweled;
not burned at the stake with the spittle of curses

sizzling on their lips like bacon fat.
A perfect record. I consider it a win

if each avoids the iron maiden,
hot coals & the rack. True,

some were sentenced to *the hole*,
though not a hole they can't climb out of

like catatonics dreaming the dreams of Usher,
unable to whisper *Help!* at their rain-slicked wakes.

Also, a few have lost *good time*,
though it would be a good time less

should they find their thumbs screwed tightly,
legs adorned by vise & flame.

& none so far have been crucified,
though many within have sin enough

to purify the world
with their absence.

The Rule Breakers

He used a dead cat
slung over a fence
as a landmark:
not an X on the map
but an ex.

◆

He told his wife fresh from surgery
"Forget your meds &
bring me my tobacco."

◆

He couldn't produce urine
for a drug screen
because drugs had messed his insides up.

◆

He was clearly insane.

◆

He wanted the punishment for his deeds
without a finding of guilt:
the Brer Rabbit defense.

◆

He didn't know what the bag contained.

◆

He was helping a friend.

◆

He just woke up.

◆

He was misunderstood.

◆

He borrowed it.

◆

He was a man, you know, &
she brushed against him
listening to his heart.

The Institutional Magistrate

He sometimes starts with the Lightening Dance
before the Dance of Too Many Questions,
his dark lips sardonic, half up &

half sly, though his humor comes off
like a comic saying, "Take my wife ...
please," when he's never been married,

which goes over the head of his audience.
The Defendant feigns calm, but he's
just seen someone walk across his grave &

spit. As the hearing begins, the Magistrate
first reads aloud the rules, a paterfamilias
before the family game of *Monopoly*.

He doesn't say the dice are loaded,
that a lonely scrap of evidence is guilt, &
silence is guilt, & admitting guilt is suicide

by death of a thousand paper cuts. He smiles,
disarming & genuine. Case form at his fingers,
rule book pushed aside, he presses

Record on his micro-cassette &
releases hungry lions: the prisoner
wields a toothpick like a sword.

Neither Here Nor There

I wake feeling absent &
yet too full of weight
as if trapped in a Zen puzzle:

How can Self erase itself?
It can't & must: Schrödinger's
cat in a toxic box

where you're the cat
or I'm the cat or someone is,
someone panicked, hopeless,

clawing his own skin
as all out of sight outside
marvel at his existence or lack thereof &

then forget. Without answers.
Without even a question.
It's like the time I went free.

Warm spring air buzzed my cheeks
like fingertips. Cut grass &
wildflowers smelled like a woman &

tickled like pepper in my nostrils.
Azure brightness haloed the set.
I cruised *I-64* astride my Harley &

said, "*Shit!* I never ride motorcycles,"
exposed the dream as I dreamt it:

the old Chuang Tzu routine

if Chuang Tzu imprisoned
wished he were a swallowtail
dreaming itself Chuang Tzu

while floating through
bars of its cage like that bird
in the song "I'll Fly Away."

In Back of the Prison Van

you see what you have seen before
& never seen

schoolboy on his vacation journey
watching for the sea to appear in the sky

or a chauffeured superstar
counting paparazzi flashing by

no longer driving one hand on the wheel
the other with cigarette dangling left

as the road rises up
to obscure the trees & wildlife

you notice a city has grown beyond your memory
another rusted back to the carcass of a buck

from signs you learn
the cost of gasoline is up

a pack of *Marlboro*s is up
milk & coffee up up up

the value of your life no more than you take in
through chain-mail protecting a window

diminutive bubbles of vision
like those that belong to a fly

passing its existence at rest atop a chicken leg
or hushed & unseen on the wall of a room

where free men plot their passions
all the crimes in their unpardoned hearts

The Prisoner's Shadow

Yawn of a stain at perpetual noon:
limp, dysfunctional under fluorescents,
the lone "suicide" light above the john
keeping some eternal flame.

Even its blackness more a blur of smudged ash
on the feet of a burned cadaver, a threadless cloak—
it reflects emptiness & apathy of its bearer &
the cynical, vise-like grip of his jailers.

It lingers at his feet like shackles & chains—steel,
unbreakable. Little more than a clown's puffed-up shoes
it looks as if its parameters were codified in law:
a punitive measure, another reminder.

It doesn't box or dance, stretch arms
upward to embrace the Divine.
So small, it's a creek one easily could leap
but never cross.

II.

Notes from the Underground

"What Right Have I to Be Happy?"

—Jean Valjean in *Les Misèrables*

I could spend hours
reading poetry to the Institutional Magistrate,
though my arguments already
have enough complications
to keep him hypnotized by strobe lights
of language, all the technical jibber-jabber
that lets my clients believe
their jailhouse lawyer really knows
how to conduct an autopsy of form.
Of course they also realize in all likelihood,
whatever rule it is, they broke it,
so just want a little mercy,
as do I. But I wear a scarf
of self-pity to match my socks
handmade from discontentment:
I lost my wife to another man,
my house to my wife,
my city to a dark wave of junky nostalgia
black as a raven's beard. Too,
my wife lost her lover's unborn child,
which made me sad for her, &
for me—which made no sense &
had me telling her God is an asshole,
praise His name (Not that it helps,
the one or the other, or the One).
Sometimes I wonder if
all at once a man must pay
for every outrageous act in a long life
as though the Honorable Circuit Judge

read every festering page
from my file & told me, "So,
you were loyal to your wife but cheated
on a 7th-grade social studies test
although you knew the answers,"
then brought his gavel down
with a thundering sigh.

"What Was Your First Day
of Incarceration Like?"

—Cody McClung

When Mr. Kurtz says, "The horror, the horror,"
he's lucky. The story's over, & so is he,
no longer trapped in his nightmare world
or the existential one. Still alive &
commencing my journey deep into the dark continent
of the future, I wrapped in a tattered baby blue blanket &
strained to shake off my past: the opiate detox
fear & trembling unlike Kierkegaard's, without a faith
in anything. In a medical isolation cell,
I paced & cursed & purged, bent over the steel john
as if I lost something there: a wedding band
or matched set of dreams. Left alone, buried alive
in a cave-in of steel & stone, I didn't possess
so much as a pen to write *I want to die!*
The real Hell isn't other people as Sartre supposed; no,
it's absence, loneliness, genuine *being-for-itself,*
like that: locked up with just the ugliness
of one's thoughts. Unable to cry, crying out
unheard, I lay face down on the cold concrete,
spying through a crack beneath the door &
praying any human foot would pass:
an angel of mercy, invisible friend,
a stranger's voice in the wilderness of night.

"But When They Drop the Bad News on You, Then What the Hell Will You Do?"

—David Baldacci, *The Simple Truth*

Say to yourself, *At least it can't get worse*, although it does.
Your victim shows, curses you with eyes swearing
your many pretty wounds are glitter glass
compared with diamonds shimmering in his skin.
"Twenty-five," the judge says, while you wonder if that's
        days
or weeks. Then in a few hours or maybe a year
your lawyer develops cancer of the ear & no longer takes
        your calls.
Your friends lose themselves to madness, heroin,
something else they caught while petting spider monkeys at
        the zoo.
By now you're so exhausted when your wife requests,
"Let's separate," your mind sighs, *Whew,*
we already have, until you figure out she's not
measuring space between but what cement she's using
for the break. All you can pray as you kneel
to gather your entrails off the floor
is, *I hope he's a priest*, so at least someone might be there
to pour the shots of liquor at your wake.

"Can They Do That?"

—Johnny Redmond

They can feed you pulverized bones
of rat, but not the eyes or hair.
They can softly submerge your face in the sink,
never the toilet without a showing of cause.
They can sing country western songs
all night off key as you try to sleep,
rap on Fridays, rhythm & blues in the afternoon,
though heavy metal would violate your rights.
They can laugh at your inadequacy.
They can kick you, but only when you're down.
They'll seduce your wife with white roses &
tales of your exploits floundering
like a bear with no arms & broken wings.
On a good day they might leave you alone
(a good day for you, for they have none).
They can spin you in a centrifuge,
dress you in dresses, dance on your grave,
can tie your shoelaces in a knot
(don't say they cannot) then lock
your fingers in a Chinese puzzle
so you struggle until you disappear,
a Theseus walking threadless into a maze.

"Was It a Sign of Good Character or a Serious Character Flaw?"

—James Patterson, *Four Blind Mice*

Confession must be good for the soles
of your feet, young man. No more
shackled marches up four flights of stairs
to the Circuit Court. God bless the process
of healing. But, did you really need eight pages
to say "I did it" twice? Could've exhaled the truth
in one long sigh, avoiding all metaphor,
lyrical choreography & paragraph/indent,
paragraph/indent. Sometimes
it's better to scribble *I love you*
inside a store-bought greeting card
than write a stylish novel about devotion
where the dream girl dies in the end.
Most folks never *get it*, favor you
for what flowers you sent in words.
Of course, your attorney understands,
wishes you were mute, reciting poetry
in the language of silence. Still,
at the time it satisfied some need
like removing a splinter from your thumb,
an eye mote, or nail through the skull.
At least I found my audience at last,
you thought as you told your narrative
from birth of tragedy to denouement
while the wide-eyed sergeant
listened like your biggest fan,

said, "Hold it, let me get this down.
Hang on, hang on…."

"Do You Know You're Being Watched?"

—C.O. Tiller

The eyes of an officer, two onyx beads on an idol,
someone's idea of a merciless god in granite.
The eyes of cameras, fixated, frozen
like neighbors watching their neighbors on the news.
The eyes of the Circuit Judge, astral yet omni-
present, seeing through others' words, a blind man
reading October's *Playboy* in braille.
The subtle, plotting eyes of inmates fitting
every action into diagrams, flow charts,
commandments & blueprints for living.
The eyes of Mother, Father, teachers, friends—
those who bear burdens & witness without
first counting the forty-one ways to say, *I am alone.*
The jade, jaded eyes in the mirror already
having seen the shattering of illusions, *The Fall*,
as in the fall of Man, the fall of Clamence in *The Fall*.
The eyes averted by a wife still searching.
The eyes of the mountain directed toward Heaven
through ten thousand Hubble telescopes of pines.
The vacant eyes of passersby behind the wheel in their beat-
up rides, looking this way & that without looking at all.
The eyes of workers too weary to see the future.
The eyes, always the eyes, of whatever men call God,
attached to eternal laughter, the Great Laugh, divinely
amused by the comings-together & breakings-apart
in this sitcom with its cast of electrified dust.

"Why Would Anybody Be Bad?"

—Kurt Vonnegut, *Jailbird*

Grit or bone, it's all just meat in the mouth.
Maybe you have to pick the lock,
maybe steal a loaf from the baker's window
(how honeydewed that fresh bread tastes
to the nostrils, to the fingertips).
Not like you haven't tried it,
sniffed the drug that life is,
peeked through your neighbor's window,
mind matrixing marvelous breasts
from a blur of pale curtains at a distance.
You want to taste the birthday cake
but can't come uninvited to the party. So,
you lean back in your lazy chair &
conjure scenes from all your favorite sins
without acting, without buying a ticket to the feast.
You try to live in a bubble, not that kid
who pulls the wings off butterflies &
grows into monstrosity, sweetly cynical smiles
luring the innocent in. You try,
but thoughts wander through gray mists
of a battlefield. It is still the *you*
that is the weakest part of you, &
the wickedest. Someone asked you once
for your definition of a sociopath.
You said, "When a man
who cares for no one else
stops caring about himself."

"Suppose He Wants to Rob—
Who Can Prevent Him?"

—H.G. Wells, *The Invisible Man*

From the moment he pulls into the driveway,
he studies the symmetrical box of the residence:
two stories of rusty brick & weak gutters,
rolling windows storm-sealed, door
strictly double-locked, on the lawn a lady
crabapple, its short, pink arms not catching the level
       above.
He makes himself a burglar in his own bungalow
       then,
frustrated, reaches for his key or garage-door
       remote.
Earlier, a big cat hidden by heightened panic grass,
he lurked in a lot at the mini-mall,
observing the zip-in & shuffle-out of patrons at the
       tobacconist,
the pharmacy, the tanning bed & adult bookstore:
he could take them—one motion, a swift thwack, &
it's off with a wallet or package containing…
what? *Society doesn't want a grocer who dreams,*
said Sartre, *for to the extent he's a dreamer,*
he's that much less a grocer. How easily the meek
       become monsters,
lacking only the boiling blood of action.
Such a man might make murder
in one transcendent vision of himself.
What keeps him contained behind the old woman
who lingers too long at the ATM?

Why does his hand tremble before the carver's fang,
revolver's booming brimstone voice, the quiet rod
        or ball bat?
When night comes, he disrobes with the ease
of a ritual prayer, creeps into bed & holds his
        lover—
sleeping—to his chest as though he's innocent
beside her. But his head is full of wonder,
a field of plowed soil sown with possibilities.
Only once he stirs from rest, gets up &
goes to check the deadbolt on the door.

"How Scap'd I Killing
When I Crossed You So?"

—Cassius in *Julius Caesar*

Made brothers in blood, the wine of two vintages
poured together in that chalice of the floor,
we were as similar as the words *hate* & *hurt*.
I offered you in sacrifice to me.
You patched your torn flesh with mine.
& how does blood leave no scent in memory
& no sound, not even a movie's effects?
Though my imprecations spoke through quiet of the knife,
in repentance, I presented my heart, my back & throat
to be plucked like a sad guitar's corroded strings,
that, too, was silent, is silence, that, too,
a song left to fade & reprise with this drum
beat of consciousness returning
slowly, slowly to the raving brain.

"And Why Did He, Himself, Feel This Guilt Somewhere Deep Inside Him?"

—Hermann Hesse,
Narcissus and Goldmund

He told her, "There's darkness in me."
She smiled & cut the drug into lines
on a dinner plate. He opened to her &
she to him, & they opened themselves to
what's possible in a world lacking boundaries.
He said, "I scare me, sometimes,"
meant it the way some Oriental fighting fish
watches its own reflection in the glass,
spreads fins, prepares for war.
She nodded like a therapist in headphones,
hearing only ambient notes & radio noise.
He spoke other words she couldn't understand:
a plea for help in a stranger's language.
He never mentioned staring at his eyes in the blade
of a knife, or how he felt a thousand tiny knives
assaulting him as he waited for release from cyan tablets,
also olive, pink & yellow. She said something,
too: words of welcome, a promise.
He should've said goodbye, & so should she,
but they were stitched together with needles &
thread—Siamese twins on a narrow lane, an escalator
descending through Dante-esque visions.
They couldn't leave. They couldn't look away.

"How and Why Did He Get Hooked on Oxycontin?"

—Dave Peyton, *The Charleston Daily Mail*

You know the feeling you get
about to walk through your front door at night
when you barely see the web
inches from your face &,
at its center, what *could* be a black widow,
some harmless little creepy
or a shadow from your own desperate psyche?
Know it? How your bones tremble like saplings &
your skin suddenly smells like hot syrup?
How you'd pull away like a hand
from a stove pot's metal handle
but you've drunk too deep from the eyes of Medusa,
can't move, so let it sear a hole in your palm?
That's how I felt all along
with people, my thoughts, the future.
Not fear—fear has reason, fear you can fight.
It's not that any more than our spider's afraid of a fly
or the strangely oppressive notion
that someday the fly will come.
It's instead how an acrobat might live,
at home on the thinnest wire
while unable to cope with &
dizzied by the touch of solid ground beneath his feet:
a sadness of sorts, if sadness had knives &
fingers with which to hold them tightly,
one against your balls, one to your throat.

"So What If Blood Was Spilled?"

—Clive Barker, *Galilee*

It's darker than it was,
smelling like sulfur: a match strike,
first miss. It tastes like sex &
has a thickness of tree sap
as if I held it in the goblet of my hand:
a great molten flow from nearly-
severed thumb & twenty stray finger cuts,
the lone three-inch puncture in my back—
just my half. The other guy's
paints its own fantasia
in Palomino patterns over ceiling,
walls, a gray sky & the gates of someone
else's paradise. So much blood,
so many pretty wounds. The stripes
write a short history of mayhem:
lines upon lines of the new language
where I'm the assassin &
also his mark, Faust &
the devil who loved him
with all the deceptive fury
of an artist.

"Has the Music Faded at All?"

—Lawrence Watt-Evans,
Night of Madness

The walls have learned a low hum—
basso, staccato—
like a tuba stuck in a wind tunnel
or so many elephants endlessly marching
around the building's perimeter.
The opposite of a canine whistle,
it marks its moans
in sensible waves setting cinderblocks atremble
in aftershocks.
A little of the shake, rattle & roll,
rockin' in the unfree world,
more twisting, less shouting
except when such a ghostly stutter
starts to push its audience
toward madness
as when, just before bed,
one hears a fragment of some forgotten song,
stays awake remembering for hours,
or regretting. That sad refrain
won't leave you &
you despise it like the grind
from an airplane's engine
or rap kids driving by
with windows down & radio up,
blasting that bellowing groove
that always beats
like a tell-tale heart.

"Do You Feel Like
We're Out to Get You?"

—Sgt. Cochran

You never look over your shoulder
to see who's lurking in shadows
of a darkened corner. There are no dark corners;
only open spaces lights reach, & eyes.
Bars a grid, a leopard's cage,
cells dreary & wide like a mausoleum
with viewfinders for studying the recently entombed,
everything is visible from angles.
No need to worry someone watches;
someone does: officers
on their semi-hourly stroll around the pod,
inmates drawn in caricature with shifting glances &
shifty minds, cameras taking careful aim
like .22s—dangerous. You get used to it
as bluegills grow accustomed to the baited hook:
a fear of getting caught, sure,
but little ones will be thrown back,
while the biggest have done it so long
they slip away unnoticed like Houdini from shackles,
straitjackets or a coffin. It's not like it was
outside: some junky in the parking lot
eyeballing your stash, blue lights
like flaming bourbon in the mirror.
Not about countering make-believe threats,
it's accommodating real ones:
embracing each like an enemy
forgiven, pinning his arms
so he can't reach for his knife.

"What's the Worst You've Seen?"

—C.O. Sparks

My first prison hung no clocks:
understanding aborted, expectations
absent one minute to the next.
A man never grasps how his life depends on time
until time forgets its measure: breakfast & lunch,
late shifts, smoke breaks, happy hour.
To interrupt the pattern erases all history.
I couldn't sleep without knowing I reached
the sleeping pause. So, I paced the cell,
a pooch awaiting his master's return
through a door he closed behind him years ago.
I stared out my window, pretending
to smell morning's dew like citrus vodka,
exhaust fumes belligerent at rush hour.
Such haunting emptiness: like being
the last man on Earth—no job to go to, or to leave;
no automatic coffee drip to start each day
like a nearby bakery's fresh-bread scent.
I'd have made a sundial from a spork
if there were a sill to set it on. Instead,
I rubbed my wrist where a watch
once clung like dogfish on a shark,
tapping my pulse to prove I existed
while I searched the sky all afternoon
for any new North Star to lead me home.

"They Didn't Tell You, Did They?"

—C.O. Crigger

They never said a word.
They said too much.
They *Thee*'d & *Thou*'d & danced a whirling waltz.
They offered me $3 off my next purchase.
They sang with a country twang about fifteen ways
to forget a love that's lost.
They chanted their curses in Russian.
They eased words past black breath
of wine & tar.
They winked as they laughed &
they blinked as they lied.
They promised to let me name my star
in nebulous space so far beyond all wishes.
They told me there'd be days like this.
They never told me there'd be days like these.
They chewed their lips to hold the secret in.
They trilled their R's in retribution.
They knew what they meant,
though they never meant to hurt me.
They launched their ideas by catapult,
battering down my door with turns of phrase.
They said "Thank you" &
"Thanks for nothing."
They often said "Goodbye"
although they rarely went away.
They never said I'd be damned,
but damned if they didn't think it.
They spoke the password.
They rattled off the lists

like a tickertape of stocks still in decline.
They drudged up all those old war stories.
They revealed the spoiler.
They twisted the plot.
They forgot to declare their intentions.
They stuttered into the microphone.
They scolded me for eating the last slice.
They yodeled with derision.
They pronounced their judgment
but mispronounced my name.
They asked why I did it.
They denied my appeal.
They whispered something
that might have been sweet nothings.
They painted my portrait in similes &
other crooked lines.
They bungled the last rites.
They tried too hard to rhyme.
They sold me a *Coke* & a smile.
They never told me anything.
They never said a word.

"What Do You Think I Should Do?"

—Lawrence Stroupe

If I were you I'd paint the outside
in still life, a freedom landscape,
utilize some post/neo-Cubist style
with angles so sharp they double back &
prick your thumb below the horsehair brush:
that blood is yours, each sting
yours & yours the added splash of flush
upon a stranger's face on canvas—
suddenly it's a stealing life,
a stage magician's secret key
to facilitate escape. "The power to create,"
said Professor Ash, "is the power to destroy."
Such power equals freedom
so the quest for power
remakes the quest for freedom
in its image. In all relationships,
said Nietzsche, exists a struggle
for power: even the act of sitting down
requires governance of will over
gravity, God & chair. Then,
that subservient chair in turn
defines its master as a portrait paints
its artist with every gasp & stroke.
If I were you I'd raise the brush,
conquer your world with crimson,
flesh tones, umber—create for yourself
an exit, a door on the left
behind the table, the feast,
the dog, the brass lamp &

the girl in back &
through that doorway
grant yourself parole.

"What Will You Do When You Get Out?"

—Janet Iman

If the moon's barbell doesn't seem too heavy in my hand;
if the feel of damp grass doesn't send me running
to hide in the dry hell of my favorite shadows;
if I'm not immediately overcome by flashbacks to the
       Bronze Age,
Black Death or *Xanadu* of Kubla Kahn; if I don't give a
       stray tom
bad luck by zigzagging dumbly across his path;
if a steel spoon or knife & fork will cuddle most tenderly
with my palm; if the stink of cars & chemical plants,
mud puddles, garbage & salve off sunburned skin
won't see me spiraling into self-conscious inner rants on
       Nature
in America; if I don't shiver; if I don't cry too often;
if I don't despise & don't forget; if I don't get lost
in a song from long before—then I'll brush the dust
from my shoulders, lean over the rail of a highway bridge &
spit upon some stream whose lightning currents
cannot be defied by guarded men.

"And, If It Comes to That, How Can Any Man Be Called Guilty?"

—Kafka, *The Trial*

The sky threw a pastel quilt over everything
the evening I was innocent. I was innocent
when night tarred hills & highways,
feathered crooked treelines with clouds.
I slept little & don't remember
what I dreamt. Perhaps dust burned
on the television's never-ending face,
that household god with tears
of 1% static from the birth of the universe.
The coffee pot stank from old *Maxwell House* &
vinegar, or maybe that was the smell
of anticipation mixed with fear.
All around me, various clocks skewed time,
each trying to nudge another by a nose.
Still that soupy August dark:
it brimmed over mountains, spilling into town,
around alleyways & in through open windows
as if to preempt a coming day;
otherwise, to bury its dead with silence.

"Who Has the Courage to Break Out?"

[found scribbled in a book]

The weightlifters cradle their comforting weights &
they are free. The basketball players are free,
lobbing burning missiles at the enemy stronghold.
Free: chess men plotting, trump throwers giving sacrifice,
arrogant watchers proudly conquering new worlds on TV.
All free. All hypnotized dancers not knowing
like dogs on stage they bark & beg for other ears to hear &
eyes to see. Why not play love songs on guitar?
Why not lasso the sun or change the color of the sky?
All become emperors in a world of one.
Loved, reborn & warm at night
they sleep again in their forgetful beds.

"How Are You Feeling Now?"

[addiction recovery questionnaire]

It's like I always say, if *you* don't feel sorry for yourself,
who will? I mean, remember
that thing that loves company? Well,
I'm company. See, it's my God-given right to wallow in
      self-
pity. Let me savor the bad times: riding the highway of lost
      love
suddenly free & still a prisoner
like a tilted poker pro with Dead Man's Hand &
all his chips in the pot. It's the sense of being trapped &
yet the seeming release to come from surrender. Ah,
alone after two decades I grow wobbly,
disoriented as if by hints at unknown flavors in glass after
      glass
of different wines. Tomorrow, hungover, perhaps
I'll learn prosperity, but tonight
I've lapped up all the bitter broth.

"So We Know Where
We Stand, Don't We?"

—Agatha Christie,
And Then There Were None

The pine-box discharge needs no locks,
cage exchanged for a soil cell,
liberty maintaining distance
for men without a mind to wander.
Get Out of Jail Free card for the soul,
begging the Devil's pardon,
two-stepping across the dance floor of the worms—
don't want to buy a ticket (everyone
hits the second loop & takes the fast slope
down to rest). At least I've got my health:
broken tooth, trick knee, the usual aches
& pains plus scars from fear & the shanks of regret.
On my CD player, I'm listening to Dylan singing
"I Shall Be Released" with its double entendre,
promise of one blessing, one curse,
though which is which & why
a prisoner can't always figure out,
fighting to slip away into moonlit mist & calm,
to break away, break out,
ride the river to safety &,
should it be otherwise,
they'd have to transport me
to my grave in chains.

"Can't You Leave a Man
a Little Shred of Dignity?"

—William Peter Blatty, *Legion*

In from the cold & stripped to the skin,
their tattoos speaking a litany of their broken hearts,
they are searched by inches, they squat & cough,
they feign to laugh at blue-black gooseflesh
parading like Shriners up their muscled arms.
Though they work without shackles
in open air outside the prison walls,
they are yet prisoners always at the mercy
of someone: the road boss, the wary guards,
the camera's importunate eye & the Assistant Warden
of Security. What it means to have "clearance,"
to have freedom without being free—they jiggle &
dance, weaving their flesh to show in their nakedness
they carry no contraband: cigarette butts
sour like wet gravel, a cell phone, joint or bag
of pills, a blade. Daily, they put on this show,
more difficult getting into their cells than out.
The Warden has declared war on the world beyond,
a despiser of its many sins, despot of sunlight &
long grass, what stays hidden, can't be contained.
It's inside the fences where men are saints,
innocent & virginal in their pinkish suits.
Out there only trouble waits in a passing car,
a woman's arms, an amber bottle left half-filled
with tears of loss some stranger wept at night.

"Who Can Ever Answer
for the Morrow?"

—Alexandre Dumas,
The Man in the Iron Mask

The Parolees return in pairs, re-
criminalized, *violated.* Their shackles
seem heavier, orange jumpsuits familiar &
dim. Weary Ancient Mariners,
they tell their tales to every passerby:
Hog again shot heroin; Randy fell
for the wrong girl, then took the fall
for her. Drugs & drinking, discord &
descent into that old darkness: a *SoCo*-&-
O.J. binge for T.J.; a lone, crumbling roach
in Junior's *Ford.* A few months back,
they sat before the Board—wide-
eyed, eager, promising reform.
Khakis pressed, hair trimmed tight,
they swore, *I'll work a steady job,*
keep clean, stay home at night. But,
night has its own allure: dirty chords
from old guitars, sweat scents while dancing,
hands that stutterstep tracing the curves &
smiles—*Lord*, those smiles: wicked &
delightful! What comes next is
the sound of laughter at sunrise
of another day. Who's laughing &
why? The Parolees won't speculate.
It's everywhere at once, surrounding &

filling them with madness
like shadows in a thunderstorm
drawing silhouettes of demons
on every wall a restless child sees.

III.

The Idiot

Status Report

I look into myself & see music
but can't hear the notes or name the song.
I look out my narrow glass at twilight &

see rain over razor wire, a river of mud
down a mountainside, nothing at all the color red,
the color of anger, of life & of suffering.

I have time enough for a novel now
though I find I have nothing to say.
I have time enough to write enough letters

to woo every single woman in the world,
but the world is too full of women
who've forgotten the sound of hunger

in my voice, the smells of fruity liquor &
desire in the whispers of my breath.
I wish I could write myself letters;

I've forgotten me, too. My God,
I'm an empty chalice next to an empty plate.
So I sleep because sleep is freedom: we say,

"I have robbed them of an hour."
I sleep because in sleep I see
endless open roads, roast turkey &

thick burgers, the faces to names I've lost.
I sleep because in sleep I see nothing
often: we say, "Through the hole,

down the hall, winding the corridor,
mapping the maze, follow the cat
in your dream—he knows the way out."

Cool, Real Cool

Convicts sometimes dream the coolest stuff:
*Harley*s, pistols, stocking masks & booze
& Angelina Jolie in the buff,

Mugshots of their best friends looking rough
On *America's Most Wanted* or the news.
Convicts sometimes dream the coolest stuff.

They sleep on bunks of steel instead of fluff
But rarely find it difficult to snooze
With Angelina Jolie in the buff.

Thus nebulous each milquetoast's walking tough
Down *For-Madmen-Only* avenues.
Sometimes convicts dream the coolest stuff.

& just when nighttime swears they've had enough,
Like junkies they fiend all day for revues
Starring lithe Ms. Jolie in the buff.

Though time dissolves their pardons in a puff
When they awaken back to bars & ashen hues,
At least they paused to dream the coolest stuff.
Oh, yes! *O, Angelina*! In the buff...!

Drug History

I didn't used to smoke & then I did &
then I went to prison where smoking was outlawed &
cigarettes were everywhere.

I drank a bit here & there & mostly there &
mostly vodka which is like drinking water
without all the impurities &
with more hope—also hopelessness.

I always loved coffee—my gateway—
started age 6 & started a pot at 6 a.m.
to give me a start come every sunrise since.

But it's the pills you want to know about—
the three *-dones* (*oxyco-*, *hydroco-*, *metha-*) &
the *-phines*, the *-phones*, the fiending—
but it's not the pills you want to know about;

it's the knives. The knives came after,
conjuring all the pretty wounds, blood lines
like a soldier's lead-shot canvas.

I'll tell you in confidence—
can you spare a *Marlboro* & a hot shot
of good old joe?—see, here's the why of it:

it's about wanting,
it's about silence, as if any-
one could hold that like a knife.

Expirations

mostly tonight I sit lamenting
the recent loss of my driver's license

not from DUIs accidents citations
so much as the weathering of time & absence

how things pass unnoticed when you're not looking
the perfect sunset an eclipse a cloud with the face of God

what can a man do without his tiny traffic pass?
how far seem the factories fields & fast-food chains

oh & how might one find life-affirming love
with even the restaurants & theaters so remote

I'm scheming on pragmatics of renewals when I first learn
about the death of Ms. Nitzi the old commissary lady

whose name the name most knew wasn't even her name
names too things that expire

all those years she sold sodas candybars & ice cream
all the sweetness those benedictions for the sugar paradise

it's whispered cancer got her
I never saw her smoke though she was young once

probably a real looker a knockout bombshell
with wild nights short skirts & dancing dancing dancing

neither her death nor this image of her life
cancels out concerns over my license

or entices forgetting how a man suffers from his own
            defeats
they only modify a moment in time already quite askew

make me ponder more the things I've lost &
the many other things I'm yet to lose

Release

without bars
still there would be sunlight

to confine me
in a box of shade

I want the freedom
midnight offers

to walk along the Ohio River
swimming in the stars

I beg Your Honor's
pardon

to put aside
the penitentiary

to disregard
the day

I am lonely without
a moon's solemn mouth

warning me
wooing

a glaring goodbye
a soundless lullaby

Letter to the Parole Board

I am not innocent
not the atomic clock that keeps perfect time

I stole fire from the sun &
gave it to Man for his sustenance

I deserve the rock
the chain & the eagle

when the last voice on the wind cries out
it is my name that voice condemns

freedom is the Springtime smell
of wildflowers by the highway

I've not tasted that soft perfume along a neck
in centuries beyond my reckoning

at what point does the ground absolve
the pride that comes with flight?

how many times must I push this boulder uphill &
laugh at myself as I watch it roll back down?

I know you are not merciful gods
though within smolders a spark of the power of mercy

I ask it of you

I am not innocent

but deeply censured by my years of strain
only so long can I bear aloft the sky

Flight of Fancy

when a convict
dies

a vulture escapes
from the paper bag

that once
held meat

now only a burn-
scarred blood-

soaked feather's thorn
remains

Dust

It floats through air like rabbits in zero-G,
tiny feet squirming, pistons pumping,
finding no ground to guide their wingless flight.
A polar bear carpet, it softens stone flooring
beneath my bunk. "Don't think of it,"
says the professor of philosophy &
there it is. Always. Omni-
present. It burns the nostrils like diesel fumes &
infiltrates hair—a nation of velvet lice.
Some of its molecules once were mine:
ashes to ashes & dust to everything else.
Teardrops from a sandstorm's eyes;
loincloth for a sleeping giant;
in a phantom's ring, the jewels—
it's the garbage of existence &
in a cup of wind it is the wine.

Possible Side Effects

alprazolam (*Xanax*) numbs burdens & what pizzazz
blue skies brightly bluster dulling even distance between say
cocaine & codeine so different in nature yet how they tax
darkness then lead to darkness in the soulless hollow
end you can swallow snort smoke shoot an IV
fluid drip until you yourself drip into fluid or burn with flu
God can't make up his mind between pleasure pain & whatnot
Heroin for example the big H is so like kiss-
ing a mermaid on her fishy lips as the tide's mean roar
jags at you knifelike & powerful slashing the EQ
killing the woofers & tweeters in your head *pop pop pop*
loud as caged-baboon screechings at the Pittsburgh Zoo
methadone helps softly refocusing the opiate lens within
now that you're trying to stop trying to get away from
Oxycontin siren songs with their constant heavenly pull
pulling pulling toward the next hell the next kick
"Quit" your friends tell you "Put it down" as if a glass of OJ
right nothing's that easy with benzos goofballs junk booze I
shit you not Iranian revolutionaries overthrowing the Shah
took less time & effort to place their hated pig
under the ax & we haven't even touched on crack or crank if
*Vicodin*s & *Valium*s won't do the two small C's release
wickedness within enough to make you wish you were dead
Xed out shuffled off this mortal coil tracing the end of your arc
yes you've run out of options now a mindless blob
zero chance you'll ever be a good son to your mama

Wake Up

I miss the sound of your nightmares
breathing through black like whispers of bat wings.

Sighing at first, a whimpering pup, you'd shutter
neck to ankle like a picture of a radio wave.

If I caught you then, saved you
from maniacs, spiders, fear of infidelity,

if I touched fingers to your cheek,
you'd gasp like Houdini's crowds

upon his reemergence from the tank
when he gave them back their breath.

Otherwise, you made yourself the monster:
groaning, roaring, spouting demonic curses

untranslated from the language of sleep.
Sometimes there was weeping,

sometimes a hiss. I liked to watch you,
love, more vulnerable than naked in the tub:

the quiver in your eyelids, lips tapping
S.O.S. in Samuel Morse's code.

You smelled like sweat & roses,

anxiety misting off your skin.

Mostly, love, I wanted to be the one
to wake you, quiet your creaking tongue.

It was my face, my voice that fed you
repose, eased you out of danger

as your heartbeat lowered, brain reset,
before you returned wherever it was I wasn't.

Tell Me

for my mother

tell me again the story of the Mexico trip with father's
exploding retread tires smuggled tequila driving gloves & shades

tell me go to bed early & wake up late
so dreams will have their hours to germinate

tell me you keep memories like mementos in their labeled crates
tell me you named a holiday for your first love's date of birth

tell me about your travels—does zinfandel in Boston
beat out cabernet in Chicago or a silky mango daiquiri down south?

tell me get a better job live hard stop wasting your life
tell me days like this turn into years like these

tell me a good disaster tale: how wind took the shingles &
lightning the tree & cousins always seem do die in threes

tell me it's possible to reflect without regretting
tell me how to shovel snow in Spring

40th Birthday

Watch for the unusual, discarded and
forgotten to provide some tasty opportunities.
—horoscope for Libra

8 cups of coffee 2 roast beef sandwiches
1 sudoku 1 headache 4 white ibuprofen tablets

listen to Mike Doughty's *Golden Delicious* CD twice
255 shuffles setting up 51 games of solitaire

lost & won everybody faces growing old alone
decked with hollow numbers like motley crooked balloons

8760 hours until the next one comes around
may the 1 God bless this cluttered heart

Death Notice

Copper reads only obituary pages:
bold names, blurred faces
in black-&-white photos,

hometowns, survivors, litanies
of acts meaningless from the context
of history. He mines each block

in search of sighs & recognition,
nostalgia for the familiar once it's gone.
Leaning onto his pillar of bones

like a scholar studying Aristotle,
trying to penetrate densities
of the *Metaphysics*, meta-

something—what comes after—
all lives defined by awareness of death,
Copper embraces that self-

knowledge in ends of others like Hemingway
on his French hotel balcony
reading about his own demise,

sometimes laughing, sometimes grateful
for words he doesn't see
upon the page.

Taken Away

i.

Love is the empty bunk, the blank space
announcing desolation of a man condemned
twice: for his crime & his tenderness.

ii.

All that's lost to us is another inmate, a survivor
with his dumb smile & notebooks filled with song lyrics.
To him, it's the river at night on its long drift toward the
      sea.

iii.

They packed his things, took him in cuffs from his cell.
"You know what it's about," the Corporal said. He knew.
A man can't love a woman & not expect to suffer.

iv.

Who was she? An employee, a teacher
who educated him with soft caresses, careless words;
a ghost by mist-light seen through prison glass.

v.

The empty bunk will not stay so for long—a day, maybe
      two.

Its new occupant cannot speak of love's resourcefulness &
        cost,
his eyes averted from the past, heart a cruel jailer for desire.

In the Dayroom

the prisoners watch a movie about prison
not the classic where Tim Robbins escapes

or Clint Eastwood escapes
or Tom Hanks puts the innocent man to death

instead it's Eddie Murphy
who can't escape Martin Lawrence

or his own misfortune &
can't protect his cornbread

the cons laugh wildly
children overcoming fear of clowns

morbid slapstick & masquerade
as if they haven't seen it

patients in a cancer ward
viewing DVDs of their MRIs

Midnights

I lie awake at midnight
with my arm around the memory of you.

Midnight is not midnight
without the song of your breath on my neck,

tastes of your sweat & perfume—
unfermented grapes—upon my lips.

If only the moon hung lower in the sky
or wind hummed different melodies of peace,

other midnights would have filled me with stillness,
a pause from arguments, intensity & rage. So,

I lie here in silence like an unspoken apology,
unable to sleep when the sound of rain

reminds me of you, & cooled, comforting air
reminds me of you, & everything else, however sad or soft,

reminds me I'd drown a thousand midnights in the sea
to recreate just one I spent with you.

Property

All I own fits in a box & a bag.
All I have loved engages the rage of rockets
                              blown bright &
            quivering back as dust,
                        the scattering, descent & darkness.
For want of a dollar I'd insert one poem
            into a vending machine for peanuts:
                                    the mechanism
                  washes it back as counterfeit.

How would it be to possess an interest in the sun,
a lien on my lover's breast, a trove of what bonds
            best mature like words of light & warmth
            against the blank, blurry skin of winter's page?

Law books call it *Blackacre*, some hypothetical
property that can be bought or sold for a peppercorn.
It has its rules—so many, a litany of the possible,
gospel of ownership.
                              Oh,
                  to profit from such fiction....

I must give back my tee shirts, underwear & socks.
My belt shall tie pants to a stranger's waist.

I hold my plot in the family field,
                              a black acre.

Otherwise, it's just the sound of rain on remembered
            rooftops;

nostalgia for clowns & shopping malls,
            lost pets, spontaneous laughter &
      eavesdroppings splattered on the unrecorded past.
There's so much nothing in the world: a man can't even
      own that
            without acquiring something in the loss.

Guilt

completely inappropriate for me to say to you
your lower back's a scroll on which the sweetest words are
      written

to end my mournful lonely monologue with *nymph*
in thy orisons be all my sins remembered

it would be wrong describing the way your breasts
beneath a tight green sweater etch a sacred shadow

from my profane longing
when you lean across the desk

a shapely silhouette reaching toward me
as though to place the irons on my wrists

I have made a prison of holding my tongue
I have made a prison inside the prison already in my heart

still you smile & cover your mouth when you laugh
as though we were intimates

but the time is not right for *how-do-I-love-thee*s
when speaking *Thou* in penitent silence

stretches least the skin of expectations
it would be a dangerous mistake

to promise you anything so I will not promise
though the offer lingers in this unsigned plea

The Feeding of the Birds

it is not that so much bread is wasted
why this is prohibited

for these tiny finches bland & gray as businessmen
the occasional portly pigeon slight-flying with a wobble

neither because they chatter & cluster
nor shit on windshields of the warden's cars

it is not because they sing &
in singing raise the spirits of the dead

not the companionship they offer
fleeting as a naughty girl's at night

one never need examine too exactly
their piercing abysmal judge's eyes

or the soft dance steps
their tiny legs will disco toward the feast

it is because they enter & exit so freely
through the fence without restraint

that gives men hope
where naught should be but suffering & remorse

Creative Writing

Out there I wrote poems
for friends who enjoyed a vision
with pinches of passion &
just a dash of melancholy. Here,
I'm asked to write letters—
deviant, hungry, decadent with spice—
meant for lovers safe in their freedom,
women I've not met.
A jailhouse Cyrano sans desire,
I'd much prefer whispering
lines on the narrow view
outside my window. *Less moon*,
my patrons plead. *More cocks &*
cunts. Each wants his girl to know
he is smacking her ass
in his sleep, so she gasps … again,
crying out from his astral touch. *But*,
I say, *I'm better at making her sigh*
perhaps, or sing. To which each tells me, *Yes!*
That's exactly what I want,
although it isn't.

Blame

give me all of it
the heat from the sun

the torn curtains
the cat that died of age

heap on me
those layers of bricks

to build my sorrow house
with its chambers of regret

your lousy job my fault
your rundown *Chevy* mine

your alcoholic father
I poured his first drink

& his last
if ever it comes

the tumors on your uterus
I cut you open by moonlight

my needlework swift
stitching curses

there
& there

it's not enough
give me more

the long grass
rain pouring through the roof

your lover who left you
the hearses that mar your view

as they circle
round & round your home

in ugly parade
for a terrible holiday

Apology

To the misspent motorcyclist, whose misfortune
left him sideswiped by a young mom in a minivan,
for whom I didn't stop as he spun like a bag of serpents

when I passed him in the road; to the couple by another
        lane
standing beside their *Subaru* lit up like a jack-o-lantern's id,
a rage of flame in my mirror; to a homeless, hungry vet

in Huntington to whom I gave three quarters
that easily could've been six or eight & that other dark-
eyed vagabond perhaps a saint in Pittsburgh, whose

outstretched arm I ignored because he frightened me
as if the ghost of my lonely, alcoholic grandpa;
to the girl with whom I shared my pills &

to the girl with whom I shared my cocaine &
to the girl who shared my shots of vodka straight,
spiced *Bacardi 151*, assorted whiskeys & beer,

the madness of the a.m. that comes on like
some unseen rock beneath a mower's blade;
to the groundhog in Martinsburg I ran down,

whether speeding or not; to the Amish man I cursed
beneath my breath as he rode his hearse-
like buggy down a narrow Pennsylvania mile;

to all the truck drivers I have flipped the bird
for cutting me off then slowing on a hill; to children
I've frightened at Halloween by leaving my grass long

as a witch's hair & all the windows blinded,
house so eerily dark; to my parents for whom
I've caused too much grief to speak of;

to the mutt I barked at when he often barked at me;
to the dead I never mourned; to those I've wronged &
then forgotten like pebbles in a lengthy gravel road—

may mercy rise within you like a sourdough loaf,
may forgiveness reanimate from its silent grave:
once we embraced like two arms in a straitjacket,

held each other closer as enemies then—now,
I would meet you as a friend on this sacred journey
to a shrine we've built for our miserable nostalgia.

Watching the Steelers
Win the Super Bowl

Moments shaved like sawdust from my time:
I blinked & woke in a sunlit field, limbs &

hopes as free as eagle wings. No opaque metal sky,
no cage, no numbers that shackle men

to a place like cattle brands. One can forget
what prison *is*, that it exists at all as more than some

promised mind-beast of bad little boys.
One can, & I was one

note lost in the melody of a song only I could hear.
Though my next day would mean no more

than long hours carved like ugly monuments
in stone, for a while, unpardoned or furloughed,

I escaped the walls that held me
like curses from an angry god.

The Chaplain at Night

Hardest hearted stone men, dark-armored in mail of blue tattoos,
their muscles swollen clouds of burning rain, eyes fierce &
glassy as gems for a granite demon—how they weep

when the chaplain comes at night. Whenever the chaplain comes at
        night,
the sight sounds a banshee's shriek, maracas from a rattler's tail,
what refrain some unseen pistol sings like a squeal of brakes on the
        highway.

Everyone longs to turn away, instead looks on with awe that fear
        assigns
as if fixed to the sofa & forced to endure a month of 9/11
or war coverage on the TV news that never changes.

All want & don't want data, information, facts: whose
lot was drawn, whose name highlighted in the book of suffering?
Someone's sainted mother, faithful wife or infant child

just fell beneath the wheel of ambivalent fate, body crushed like
        bones
of an enemy. Someone's tether to a happy life, a free world
        snapped.
Though the chaplain speaks words of faith & hope, those words

reek from a freshly dug grave, wet earth, pungent roots of grass &
onions, dead smells the dead smell: by being there
he breaks a man—being there, how easily it happens.

Bad Day

I lose gambling
how many bones

will break
before I scream.

Armed Robbery

Give me your jewel-encrusted,
pleasing words & promises of redemption,
hope, or I shall excommunicate
your second soul from its church
of skin & bone.

              The ski mask is essential
              for all attempts at self-parody;
              blond wig & clown nose, optional.

Hand over the pork rinds, Pal, &
those old copies of *Weekly World News*
or I will surely punch a hole
in the space/time continuum
with this superconducting supercollider,
discrete travel size.

              Penalties enhanced for firearms;
              knives less menacing but, *boy*,
              can they cut through butter.

Please pass the salt, Mother,
or I shall not be so polite
the second time.

              False tags: maintain
              for the getaway car. Obey
              traffic laws. Only make left turns.

Give me chastity &

continence, O Lord,
or else...!

The Perfect Murder

"Gas explosion," says the shorter of the two inmates—
sad smile, greasy Elvis hair—& you can tell he's
considered it, measured the hiss & stink, the spark,
though why & for whom he doesn't let slip.
"Hole in the line," he says, "then *Boom!* It burns away all
       trace."

Nothing the other suggests seems as interesting:
car wreck, sleeping pills, several other versions
of fire like smaller-caliber bullets
without the bright & bloody big bang of their betters.
Even this back & forth is tense as a Hitchcock film,

so I interrupt, interject, "No,
the best weapon's still a deadly scorpion.
You can't get fingerprints off a deadly scorpion"—
a set-up, waiting for the question.
Finally, the taller one gives in:

"Why can't you get fingerprints off a scorpion?"
he says. I say, "Because it doesn't *have* any fingers,"
as the hard, embarrassed silence of one &
Tommy-gun laughs of the other
reshuffle their dreadful Tarot deck of a dialogue.

It's like that scene in *Psycho* when you
first realize it's Norman Bates wearing his mother's clothes
       &
you don't know whether to giggle, gasp

or softly readjust your ashen wig
as you sink down lower, ever lower in your seat.

The Performers

The guards would not permit a man to sing
as shackles chimed their percussion on the stairs.

The bailiff dismantled laughter with an elbow's joke
told to tender flesh where breath would fix its humor.

The judge gagged all honeyed lips, &
even the deputies muffled their mutterings

so as not to be misunderstood or mistaken
for poets overcome with wild, immortal voice.

The jury convened quickly & without theatrics
while the prisoner practiced the penance of a mime.

The jailers, meanwhile, played parts to perfection.
Oh, how the warden could dance: he could dance

like Kelly in the studio rain, a disco queen on stage;
he could dance like snow on razor wire,

grease from bacon skipping across its pan.
He completely stole the show from the executioner

who read a book once—in middle school—&,
unable to apprehend why George shot Lenny in the head,

ripped out the pages one by one & fed them
like a hundred uncollected bodies to the flames.

The Prisoners

i.

All faces gray,
the gray
of cinderblocks
& steel, gray

of dust on a checkerboard,
gray of dust
in a cloud of dust
as it settles.

They have seen too much,
smudged the flush
from embers
of memory's freedom,
covered them up
with ash.

ii.

Gray lines
on their gray faces

spin threads
like spider's silk.

They rise
& fall
with willful slowness
of a smoker's
gray exhale.

iii.

What does it mean
to hope?
To want more
than this?
To dream
of the outside,
then forget?

If, then, an
omnipotent God,
can He
sentence a man
to a term so long
he shall never
be released,
then release him?

iv.

Gray the eyes
attuned to God
as they read
& reread
pages of the Word
that blur
into gray.

A man sees
only what he wishes,

a closed door
without a key
when really
it's a key
without a door.

v.

Loneliness!
Loneliness.

Their wives
have taken lovers
in the name
of forgiveness.

Their children
have taken
fathers
in the name
of forgetting.

vi.

Gray of thunderstorms
seen through glass,

gray of the mountain
by mist-light,

the gray of tomorrow
& the gray of yesterday,

gray of the knife,
the gray of the knife

when the blood
is wiped away.

vii.

Ye, though I walk
through the valley
of the shadow of gray...

Songs of the mountain
are gray as walls,
gray as fences
& razor wire,

gray as the rec yard
& the gray of weights.

At night
there is silence
but there is
never silence.

About the Author

Ace Boggess was locked up for five years in the West Virginia prison system. During that time, he wrote the poems collected here and published most of them. Prior to his incarceration, he earned his B.A. from Marshall University and his J.D. from West Virginia University. He has been awarded a fellowship from the West Virginia Commission on the Arts, and his poems have appeared in such journals as *Harvard Review, Notre Dame Review, Southern Humanities Review* and *The Florida Review*. His first collection, *The Beautiful Girl Whose Wish Was Not Fulfilled*, appeared in 2003. He currently resides in Charleston, West Virginia.

BRICK ROAD

POETRY PRESS

Our Mission

The mission of Brick Road Poetry Press is to publish and promote poetry that entertains, amuses, edifies, and surprises a wide audience of appreciative readers. We are not qualified to judge who deserves to be published, so we concentrate on publishing what we enjoy. Our preference is for poetry geared toward dramatizing the human experience in language rich with sensory image and metaphor, recognizing that poetry can be, at one and the same time, both as familiar as the perspiration of daily labor and as outrageous as a carnival sideshow.

BRICK ROAD
POETRY PRESS

Also Available from Brick Road Poetry Press
www.brickroadpoetrypress.com

Dancing on the Rim by Clela Reed

Possible Crocodiles by Barry Marks

Pain Diary by Joseph D. Reich

Otherness by M. Ayodele Heath

Drunken Robins by David Oates

Damnatio Memoriae by Michael Meyerhofer

Lotus Buffet by Rupert Fike

The Melancholy MBA by Richard Donnelly

Two-Star General by Grey Held

Chosen by Toni Thomas

Etch and Blur by Jamie Thomas

Water-Rites by Ann E. Michael

Bad Behavior by Michael Steffen

Eulogy for an Imperfect Man by Maureen A. Sherbondy

Rising to the Rim by Carol Tyx

Treading Water with God by Veronica Badowski

Rich Man's Son by Ron Self

BRICK ROAD

POETRY PRESS

About the Prize

The Brick Road Poetry Prize, established in 2010, is awarded annually for the best book-length poetry manuscript. Entries are accepted August 1st through November 1st. The winner receives $1000 and publication. For details on our preferences and the complete submission guidelines, please visit our website at www.brickroadpoetrypress.com.

www.ingramcontent.com/pod-product-compliance
Lightning Source LLC
Chambersburg PA
CBHW031856090426
42741CB00005B/518